Jean Atkin

How Time is in Fields

Best wishes,
Jean Atkin

Indigo Dreams Publishing

First Edition: How Time is in Fields
First published in Great Britain in 2019 by:
Indigo Dreams Publishing
24, Forest Houses
Cookworthy Moor
Halwill
Beaworthy
Devon
EX21 5UU

www.indigodreams.co.uk

ISBN 978-1-912876-07-5

British Library Cataloguing in Publication Data. A CIP record for this book can be obtained from the British Library.

Designed and typeset in Palatino Linotype by Indigo Dreams.
Cover design by Ronnie Goodyer from image 'Croplands' by Claire Scott www.clairescottsite.wordpress.com.

Printed and bound in Great Britain by 4edge Ltd.

Papers used by Indigo Dreams are recyclable products made from wood grown in sustainable forests following the guidance of the Forest Stewardship Council.

for Mary Anderson Atkin, 1928-2017,
who read landscape to me

Acknowledgements

Many thanks to the editors of the following books and journals where some of these poems first appeared: Agenda, Ambit, Magma, Coast to Coast to Coast, The Moth, Lighthouse, The Interpreter's House, Under The Radar, Northwords Now, Island Review, Pushing Out the Boat, Earthlines, Prole, And Other Poems, Zoomorphic and Ink, Sweat and Tears.
'The tattoo'd man' was placed 3rd in the Prole Laureate Competition 2015. 'How strange we are' was Commended in Battered Moons Poetry Competition 2015. 'Jacob McCullough's holy barrow' won the Fire River Poets Competition in 2014.
'Chough' was commissioned by Sidekick Books and 'Regarders of the forest' by Worple Press. 'Eglwyseg day' is published in Waymaking, edited by Helen Mort, Claire Carter, Heather Dawe and Camilla Barnard, from Vertebrate Publishing. 'One uncertain history' was commissioned by Ledbury Poetry Festival in partnership with Malvern Hills AONB for their 2018-19 project 'Troubadour of the Hills'.

My thanks especially to friends and fine poets Steve Griffiths and Heidi Williamson, and to all in Border Poets for good lunches and wise suggestions in the making of this book. Love as ever to Paul, Lenny and Dougie.

CONTENTS

How Time is in Fields

almanack i

maedmonath

the meadow-month
all hayseed and diesel, us
crosslegged on the rocking
stack of bales

weodmonath

in the weed-month
kneeling, back-bent
we ease out creeping buttercup

behind us, our dusted toes

haligmonath

the holy-month
when the weeks turned green
and full of paths

How we rode after haytiming

Soft weft of halters slapped our sides in our dash
to the paddock for the fastest.
Then the calling and the catching,
ponies wiry-lipped at pockets.
We led them out through a gate hinged on string

and slid the slippery shine of bareback
fingers twisted into manes, neck-reined,
fast trotting up the track
for tack, leaned back against the jolting, the joking.

Then in Long Field we were sharp and skinny
on hard old saddles,
greyed our knuckles on flashing shoulders.
Out on the stubble, squinting at sun, we held the yaw
and flare of ponies in their weaving line –
tightened the rising lightness on the bit
          – till a shout
                    hairtriggered them to flight –

and with stomach's lurch of thrillful risk
and roaring air in underwater ears –
we hurled our ponies
full belt down the light.

Nettle lexicon

1 nettle of the edgelands

So, the nettle dare – will you grip that hairy leaf?
Stand still and rigid for this ordeal
while they wait in a circle and watch your face?

2 nettle of the dens

Sharp flare of weals rising white on your skin,
a dapple of pain you soothe to a green smear
of dockens. Scrub-leaf. In dock, out nettle.

3 nettle of the beds

Older, gloved and kneeling, you hang and draw the soil
for them, their creamy guts, the hoary coil and pack of them.
Them snapping, whipping back to test you.

4 nettle of the gone

O how the nettles do grow behind us, markers
for our wiped-out villages, abandoned farms.
How rife they are in the lost places.

Eglwyseg day

[11.09 am]
path up through windclipped gorse, wind in the eye
and such yellow splashes through the heather

sheep-cropped mounds and sink-holes of the mines
smooth as china cups and saucers stacked up

at the table edge
and shelved up there, the purple hills,
here, bilberries and our purple fingers.

[12.23pm]
coffee from the Thermos. Perch
on springy bones of heather root and watch

across the gorge, a nursery
of dark firs gathered quiet
and good by the cliff's white knee

we listen to the nudge
of a sheep through whinberries

                    and hum of a bee-line into warm air.

[1.53pm]
path divides into two green trails. We know
we have chosen the right way when

we can look down on the other as it narrows to a thread,
full-stopped at a brink by a sleeping sheep.

Berries are red-dangled, plumping above pale screes.
We halt by a jut of stones

where a twist of swallows dives and feasts
on insect-clouds blown

from Eglwyseg's lips.

[2.45pm]
beyond: raised tide of Llantysilio's hills
near: like a little adder striped and scaled

a brown caterpillar inches in the dust.
Spent thistles, dying in their upright stalks

and at our backs the moor rolls up to Ruabon,
above a gleaming weave

of thistledown, loose cloak of looms and
riddles.

[3.03pm]
fresh gulley water bubbles in a sink
of stone, then falls and empties back

inside the hollow hill. It leaves no sound.
We walk past a vole passage drilled through dung.

A fence-line stitches the grouse moor. Eyes stop
on a fencepost with tilted crow.

Bronze Age burial kist, mapped once,
gone now.

[3.56pm]
spreadeagled by the wall, a dead sheep, chalky
porous vertebrae in rainwashed fleece

we pass three daisies low along the path, like dropped
white pebbles from children's pockets

and the mountain rears and grins,
shows all its caried limestone teeth.

In yellowhammer weather

Before the beech nuts have tumbled
into the ramparts,
before Frank's stockbook
is not needed,

(she'll tie it with ribbon,
place it in the dresser)

Polliwig trots in The Harp.
He arches his crest and picks up pace
as the brown Clun winds.

Who can stop time?

Frank takes the green lane on his favourite horse.
The hedges are loose, meet over their heads.
Polliwig's dapple shines on his shoulder.

Frank's Clun sheep rub their backs on the boles.
They brace their hooves between thin-fingered roots
and rake their rumps.

Polliwig bounds the track to the tump,
grey horse in grey sky.
Frank darns the pigwire with binder-twine

looks over Clun and Unk and Kemp
and listens by the wheat
and a coppice of ash
for *a little bit of bread and no cheese*

Makes Polliwig stand,
as horses stand, like days.

The breaker

Colts and fillies trembled on long reins.
Tha'll be steady pet, now then, he said
and leaned his brow to theirs.

He wore blue overalls slapped by cows' tails
and torn check shirts. He had cattle cake in his pockets.
He had a bad knee and split wellies.

I followed him over the ruts of Hardland to watch
his swollen hands as soft as sheepswool on the ropes,
the ponies learning to listen.

He was drizzle off the fell and frayed rope halters.
He was a comfrey poultice and strong tea.
He was the running horse under the hill.

I learnt to back them, quiet as owls,
while he steadied them and held their heads.
I learnt to murmur to them, watch their little ears.

The dog days of Dumfriesshire

23rd July
A bee flies under
thin weaves of grass
where she lies flat, fifteen.
It disturbs the spiny seedheads
and flies on. It seems
so purposeful.

tall sky duck-egg blue scud cloud winds easing

30th July
She wishes to sleep dreamless
by the garden pond
where the lives of frogs
are full of luck. Instead,
below the marigolds,
she discovers a dim paradise of beetles.

long sky arsenic green with mottled cirrus humid

7th August
Chicken shit and lichens dot
dry concrete flags. Self-seeded
into the cracks, the tender
leaves of columbines.
She paints her toenails
carefully, and pink, above the dust.

bowl sky Palnackie blue cloudless hot

19th August
Lawn grass too long uncut
is bent, bead-spangled.
She watches a droplet
quiver at a tractor burring up the brae.
There's no reason to wait around.

cranefly sky   *hammered silver*   *high altitude nimbus*   *no wind*

23rd August
The baler's stuttered rap
loses ground to the tow of a warm front
spooling in from the Atlantic.
She goes back to the wheel
of a red kite, like a thought
on a thermal, before storms.

galvanised sky   *loss-grey*   *mares' tails*   *heavy rain*

Oystercatchers

I squat down by his still-perfect stripes.
Lift him, warm but gone,
find the vehicle has wrecked the other side of his head.
Try not to look in his ruined eye.

A robin and a blackbird sing, a tractor stumbles
half a mile away. I carry him home,
planning a shovel, thinking
what words can take his place.

After school he's stiff and changed. Our children white
with shock, they've not yet seen the death
of something young.
We stand in Wood Field round a grave.

The nights are drawing in, it's getting late.
I lay him good eye up.
Their tears stream on and on over the hills.
They trickle into drystone dykes.

Up there the clouds are dark and racing.
Here, we are in this day.
For keeps, in all our heads, the sobbing and
the oystercatchers whistling.

this netted house

flounders in the breaker-air, is leaning
gale-drunk on the singletrack

wind cracks like a sheet this morning

pink sandstone soft and ashlared
snared in black-mesh net

part-boarded windows flash fish-eyed

tied at the footings of each fret
stone-wall can't lean, can't swim

with the current to the brim,
can't crash in the tide

tin roof is a banging in the ears

snagged in light-blue nylon squares
red oxides bleed and disappear

door held shut on a twig through a hasp

this house roped down is anchored
to the land's grasp

Eliza in Lordshill after noon

Eliza barefoot by the chapel gate, out of bounds
and late. Her hand is on the warm iron finial. Ears full
of the roar of bees on thistles. Belly empty.

On the white lane a dog is jogging home. Two acres back
ring voices from the farm. Eliza walks the root-heave path
between the graves. Her toes discover pools of cold yew-shade.

Chapel's shut but what she's after is the cottage and a cadge.
She walks by bee balm, avens. Clouds of butterflies rise up
but no-one home. She taps again at the panel.

And feels time stand. Thinks, *this* is now. Her hand
is stopped on warm peeled paint. She tries to recognise
her fingers by their dirt, and by the sky-hung sun.

By her thumb a shadow shapes a nest deep in the leaves.
Eliza presses in through sudden dark. And all together,
nestlings
thrust up their wrinkled necks, and stretch their gapes.

Mason bees

mason bees prospect
this warm red wall

bee-buzz the same in all
the summers since

this clay was dug

into toasted crevices
and cracks of firing
they sing then vanish

Gabriel in Brook Vessons

He sets himself against the night as last light goes.
He works by rack of eye. Already the footings laid and trued.
Hand finds the stone for the space.
He's got his second wind in his second working day.

He labours, grunts as he lifts, but heart beats for this spot,
its chance, its coppice-ground, its green. Hands help him
as they raise the wall. He marks it's now as
black as mineshafts under-hill but just the same

and in one night he'll fettle this stack to scratch at sky.
He'll smoke out stars. Rain keeps off and woolert calls.
Selina brings a flask of tea wrapped round in cloths
and string to keep it hot. They're laying flat the hearthstone.

Under Plough and Giant's Belt he builds the chimney up,
in red re-purposed bricks he's carted here for weeks.
In sooty darkness Gabriel runs with sweat, thinks *Verily,*
what Minister says, *Verily, except a man be born*

of water and of spirit, he slathers limey mortar on,
he cannot enter into the kingdom. How Minister
pressed him deep into the river's grave.
Even a jagger can wish his one-night house be blessed.

Mynd lets first light creep down its bulk.
Selina lights the peats and first smoke wavers up
from what he's made. They raise a song. Selina strokes
her hearth and then his face and this – is living, this is.

How time is in fields

Back of Wright's Yard I climbed the 1st gate
into Spring Well. Cows cudded
& sunned by a veteran Ash.

Grasshoppers chirred in Little Rye Croft.
I turned back from a track
choked with Thistles & Sheep dung.

Little Lane Piece was sprung with Oaks.
I wound my way on a narrow path
through high Hogweed & stinging Nettles.

In Rye Croft Coppy, a Mole turned mortal,
upside to heaven. Above him brown Ringlets
wavered the Clover.

A whispering Ash at Broomy Rye Croft.
The Ragleth was rising from cover. Blue Flies
moved slowly & thickly in shade

old path swayed from tree to tree.
I crossed a dark, July-slow stream.
My way was edged with Burdock & Barley.

A scatter of Feverfew, pearly in the rough.
Wenlock Edge stepping by on my right,
long lip after lip dropping dim in the sun.

The Ragleth ran closer, slope-shouldered
& dun. Manes of Elderflower
flowed in the hedge.

At the 3rd ford, Rabbit bones, a trim of Birds,
a trembling shade like water. I climbed & had
to stop for breath. Dried mud. Hoofprints.

I climbed again. The pigments of Oak-leaves
were breaking down in dust. At the top a gate
where a great coppice-Ash marked an edge.

Now a long, green ride. Ledges of the Mynd
slept in folds at my back. Long
purple Foxgloves tilted among Hazels.

At eye's rim the Gaer Stone winked
from Hope Bowdler: volcanic watcher,
path marker, ancient fist.

I walked on the lie of the old track from Chelmick,
still tagged with winter-carded wool.
In the squatter village, the hedge-lines grew loose.

A sagging gate, a wheeled henhouse, my path
lost in crops. A Pigeon sloped through a wood.
Downhill, with Barley hissing on my jeans.

The road at last, tyre-tracked by heat.
In the verge, a Mullein leaned, & Meadowsweet.
Gunshot, once. Twice. Smell of dung

& dead stock. Crow. By Roger's Rough,
a one-eyed cottage under renovation. Everywhere
the local ground makes shift for the duration.

almanack ii

winterfilleth

in the month of winter's moon
you'll pass through scattered rain
at the wood-edge

here's bird-flight, wrench of home

you'll splash the ford and settle to the slope

blotmonath

the blood-month
baulk of lambs, unwilling
to leave the flock

don't look
in their eyes

aerra geola

in the month before Yule

we lie down in late sun
between tumuli
before winter

19 paths through Rectory Wood

1 What's not natural grows here: chimaera trees
each a grafted ring of years on rootstock.
While from the ground, what's common rises.

2 Crow passes close and overhead,
wingtips ragging lime leaves.
We see it stretch out its claws, and back its wings
land in the shine
black shine of elderberries.

3 We move through this place as through a painting,
planting a future
in oaks. But how far ahead can we imagine?

4 Green alkanet flowers lapis blue in May and on
to soft October – commonplace,
unnoticed, underhand.

5 Yews older than iron, older than churches, old
like the tumuli under the churches, the round
stones under the stones.

6 In woods we forget things.
At the wood-edge we tell stories.
Our eyes are adapted
to canopy & vista.

7 We hold a knopper gall, learn him
crouched like an homunculus, riding
the shoulder of this green acorn.
Inside him the grub of the cynipid wasp
& inside the grub, a gall wasp egg.
The grub within the grub within the nut.

8 Magpie dip & flash. Witch cackle. Repeated.

9 Lost in the woods this bristling lime is where
the path runs out in aerial thickets.
Here foxes earth mid-air.

10 Or a path we might miss, a walk inside a lime,
a local rite, a passage climbed
by children, aunts & dogs.

11 We're here to hear water, its tumble, its all-night
gutter-beck-bubble –
Town Brook's many-centuried voice.

12 Beech compensates its lean, throws out
long branches,
counterweights slowly into wind.

13 Box-straggle marks a once-clipped gateway.
A garden in a wood.

14 We raise the garden's ghost, scare up old paths
like thinning bones through trees.

15 We shush our footsteps out again through leaves.

16 A passage of yews drink darkly from Town Brook.

17 Water runs down over rock, the sounds arranged –
high notes conjured from tumbles of small stones.
Bass resonates from slab.

18 The gravity of seven yews around a pool.

19 Still water by a Green Chapel.
Time's shuffle. A way home.

Chough

I say King Arthur did not die
pyrrhocorax pyrrhocorax, fire-crow
but was transformed into the chough

his black flight slung on ozone
his salt wings fanned
his past a breaking over rocks

I say he flew with a beak of stolen firebrands
pyrrhocorax pyrrhocorax, fire-crow
a flame torn through this watered air

and my thatch tinder
the chough an inkling
red spark in a char of reeds

O fire-crow on my sill, thieving a copper nail from me
(the headland green, sea flat as a page)
O dark bird stealing glass beads from the blue

to press into a nest of roots
and thrift, all
that glamour for an egg

He splits at edge of land the feathered wind
pyrrhocorax pyrrhocorax, fire-crow
with farandole of fire-flashed beak and feet

in Cornish, *Palores,*
the digger, driving
Tintagel-deep with that blood bill

pyrrhocorax pyrrhocorax, king under the hill

The weathering of Wenlock Priory

On this houndstooth lip
are prayers
worn thin by rain.

Amens have sheared
the prior's sandstone
to this looser wool.

A hundred decades blur
the mason's chiselled line
back into plough

sown now with lichens,
titupping like his sheep
on grainy hills.

Jacob McCulloch's holy barrow

Having cycled Jacob's hills across
the narrow spine of this peninsula,
I do wonder which
was the one where his barrow –

laden with cheap stamped plates
and bowls, a-flutter with
his holy tracts and pamphlets, not to say
further burdened by Jacob himself

– the one where his barrow gathered
too much pace for the bend
on that breathless, winter-runnelled
drop, its front wheel rattling, waggling,

all steering bounding out from
under his big hands, his eyes above
those good cheekbones stretched wide
at his moment of crash. And the crack

and split of wooden spokes and then
the sound, ongoing, printing onto air,
of breaking china. Which, they say,
you could pick from that ditch,

for years, long after Jacob
had gathered up
his crumpled tracts
and gone to God.

King for a day

On the rampart I held up
a mirror
its bevelled corners
blazoned with sun

and looked down into clouds
which unrolled
into blue. Then found I could
invert

the whole hill, the trees
suspended
from the skyline by
their roots

the shops still open
and one man
on his hands like a clown.
Parish boundaries

unravelled at
the hedgelines
and the church turned
upside down.

Knocknutshell wood

We stood on the last of the Roman fort,
and northwards the small fields rose like flags.

From half a mile we couldn't miss
the yellow bucket by the pheasant pen.

And nothing else blew in the wind, just
the bright wood of Knocknutshell

bent back from the sea,
taken root on the hill.

Then we lay on its tumble
of beechmast petals

hammocked under the speech of trees,
the telling of their loosening leaves.

To be above or below sound

The morning moon is halved
and silent.
The Dwyfor runs
and will be tides.

An oak leaf,
then a beech leaf
falls, without a sound
that I can catch.

The woods have many paths that peter out.
What don't I see?

As if invisible, a deer
steps exactly
through the yew tree roots
in front of me.

Fell daemon

she goes uphill., *Harrumph* she says and snorts out air
        her jaws are whiskered slabs of bone
mane hangs in hanks to near and off

Harrumph, she says through hairy nostrils, plunges up
        the slope and takes me with her
You wanted bold?   she picks up pace
                I do not interfere
Give me my head – she roars and off we go   she
        hoists her quarters skyward as she bucks

I sink my fingers in her coal-coarse mane
        she springs her stride on the sheep-cropped track
and if I can keep this up she's mine

I want to eat that tree she announces, hoiking
                the rein from my hand
she snatches at it, baring yellow teeth
        My tree, she says, *makes legs grow broad as trunks and*
                barked with hair, impervious to storms
        Impervious, she says again
                        she dares me

she whisks her tail and brings down clouds
        I eat them up, I blow them out, I am
the engine of cold mornings

it's then I see Fell's stolen night and packed it
                                on her back
she says it smudges just like charcoal
                        weighs like lead

she says, So *then I know I am alive –*
                        she takes the weight

A brock geology

night falls & fills the dingle with badgers

badgers pressing grasses to bent curves

they feed & drink & play they trail their

piebald noses low to flow of brook & deep

below, taste all the cold then warming rocks

red iron beneath their paws & pads

they follow glint of mica in their skulls

unlock the parish scents fling back its soil

behind their claws then shoulder one

another on towards midnight & have

no questions for their deaths

Foxwhelp

apple thickens on the branch
green skin mouth-water taut
reddening, bark-rubbed.

Young vixen perfect in a morning's
first-light orchard, her legs and belly
slashed with dew, an apple in her jaws.

This acre of uprighted wands, all stepped
with dapple-dance of ladders and
all afternoon, the baskets passed and emptied.

Now stacked off flatbeds, apples mumble
in the buckets, whimper in the press
leak juices, thin and yellow

drip through channels, brew
that rough-skinned smell
and dark taste on the tongue.

The bodger goes for a turn

The bodger whacks the lathe
with a billet, shifts the centres.
He twists the rope around the wood,
tucks it in, says, *once*
the little poppets are in bed, then I
shall go for a turn.
He lays his foot to the treadle,
leans down on the lathe.
Inside his rough billet, a spindle.
The sapling dips,
the chisel lifts,
blonde wood ringlets
over his fingers.

He talks of how sap-damp
the roughed-out stool legs are.
Three legs sit
better than four on flags.
He stacks them up to dry

says, *all bodgers work by eye,*
and have a maker's mark –
could be a ring of beads
to each chair leg.
Feel this, he says, *the legs*
aren't round.

He makes a draw-knife blink.
If you can see the light glint
on its edge, it's blunt.
Above his head, on crooked
rusty nails, the rakes hang elderly,
forgetful: tines and hoops and stails.

Walker by Uley

so long and troublesome a way to find

the Walker stops for breath and the wood
breathes leaves
on the steeps
below Uley Bury

he climbs to snaking ramparts, close
under white sky, where
the Severn stripes the flat land,
broad and pale as cloth
the track turns, drops –

in the dark lane, always look both ways

he wends low in the land
gives the nod to the badgers
whose setts spill out of its walls
so he thinks of them asleep, deep
rooted and roofed in beeches

nights, they own this road

now here's a small bird shrilling
on Cam Long Down, see it
shaking brown ash seeds
out of the branches
while behind him Uley Bury stretches

the rooks blow past over Dursley wool town

the Walker climbs a narrow green bridleway
straight, horse-dunged, takes him by a farm
where two dogs bark
and bark and a rabbit
bolts up from under his feet, up
by the ruined
isolation hospital

Downham, our islanded hill

where three centuries
of smallpox sweat
under the grass

so many things vanish without trace

Such old, old trees
the Walker watches from the track –
one is pulling up its roots,
has started moving

A traveller from Uley to Owlpen enquires of landlord John Ferebee

Home's a walk in the dark
with half a moon.
Tell me the way

why, you must go along the Green and down
the hill by Fiery Lane
until you come to Cuckoo Brook

Home is somewhere back
of me. What is it
I am trying to remember?

sir, a little further on
you will pass the Knep,
after which you will go
by Dragon's Hole

Home is the same story
we all tell. What is it
I am trying to forget?

indeed, you go next
through Potlid Green
and after that
comes Marlings End

Home is the slow abrasion
of a stout boot
and a stone step

O sir! That good sole,
at the end, will bring you
down to Owlpen.

almanack iii

wulfmonath

wolf-month comes padding
        the cold ash coppice
        it's dark

        there's a scent
of wormcasts and stars

solmonath

the mud-month slants a crow
        through bare branches

        glossy eye
to the main chance

hrethmonath

Hreða's month
        one day she's sleet-stung
                weeping, back to the wall

the next, her bright hair
        snags on the buds

Boreas

After two months, it's about hunger.
The sheep are tamer, come to call.

Just now, in snow by the byre,
a wren like a dead leaf.

Wolf bounty
Stiperstones

That year you holed up in the hills in the house
of your mother and father. The year of howl
and claw: late wolves along the border.

Their half-hid glide round Manstone Rock, their easy,
lazy lope and trap. How they'd stop like a slip
in the minute that you missed them.

Missed, in all that snow, the den in the batch
as you brought down the sheep, all press
and bleat, late in the year; in the month, late.

The winter you walked the length of their hunger,
the width of their wolf-bond. When you tallied up
their sliding eyes, their wolf-hoard of patience.

That year you put your price on their heads,
your word, your lighter purse. You,
with your teeth set against theirs.

The snow years

For fifty years it snowed and no-one thought to ask why.
They were so used to it, they became like seals
and laid down fat. Like bears
they grew a pelt on forearms and faces.

Their fashions involved the intricate plaiting of long hair
to insulate necks and ears.
The regular creak of snow was a man walking.

The flump of snow falling from porches
was a woman humming inside a drift.
In their stories, trees leafed.

How strange we are

The rock spires whooped, snow whipped
at skin and Henriette d'Angeville
wished for cucumber facecream.
When her guides offered ladders and hands
to help her, she refused. Instead pressed
her small feet to the brink of glaciers,
was resolute above crevasses.

Stood pin-neat in the whiteness, feet like a dancer's,
in her own design of pantaloons in Scottish tartan tweed.
Below them, silk stockings, and red
flannel underwear next to the skin.
The pantaloons were lined with fleece, and were, she feared,
un peu coquette; so over it all she wore a dress,
same tartan, firmly belted.

Henriette – unmarried in the snows, and forty-four –
packed a bone shoehorn, because
it was not strictly needed. In rare ice brilliance she squinted
through green goggles. She burned with thirst.
She waited weeks for the weather to clear
and recorded the catches in her heart,
the wildness of her passion
for the mountain.

Nauseous, pulse hammering, she made her guides promise
to carry her body to the top, if she died.
She cut *Vouloir c'est pouvoir* into summit ice, they hoisted her
into the dark blue sky and shouted
'You are higher than Mont Blanc!'
And she opened her hands to her icy lover,
tumbled a pigeon into the wind.
La curieuse chose que nous, she wrote later,
in her green notebook.

Anthelion

Stand here, sweetheart, and breathe
this air – but not too deep.
This morning's sharp, it's stacked
with spikes of ice.

Listen – for the crackling
of crystals in the blue. Imagine
a vast white temple flung
from ground to sky.

Taste winter on your tongue, slow fall
of ice on it that dissipates,
leaves just a halo
of itself

so cold today. We'll tuck
your scarf back round your chin.
Lean close, our faces

levelled to the sky's rim.
The sun is rising now – long bars of light
that flash around us
in this frost-ribbed air; light flits
through flat ice-crystals,
bends exactly
twenty-two degrees –

and here in front of us,
not one but three suns rise
to run like dogs
across our sky.

The snow moon

On the night the snowfields above the cottage
became bright maps of somewhere else, we
climbed up in the crump of each others' boots.

Capstones of walls charcoaled the white.
The hawthorns prickled it. And a leaping trace below
a dyke was slots of ghost deer gone into the fells.

There were rags of sheep's wool freezing on the barbs
and lean clouds dragged the roundness of the moon.
Jupiter shone steady to the south. It was so cold.

And the children threw snowballs, all the time.
My old coat took the muffled thump of them.

Night snow shirred our mittens with silk. We turned
for home, left our shouts hung out in the glittery dark.

The horseman's word

I do most solemnly take upon me
the vows and secrets of horsemanship

That Word I know but do not tell, hearing
just the gait of that worked-out Galloway,
all hard mouth and spavinned hocks.

Catch up and halter the pattering
unshod ponies, my Word in their ear –
I shall not cut it or carve it, paint it
or print it, write it or engrave it –
curry their bellies' fringe of guard hair,
grass-stained skewbald, strawberry roan
Royal, Misty, Dandy, Cherry,
my Bobby Dazzler bonny filly.

Here's to the lad that can always conceal
And keep a thing hidden
Now the words go, like snow off a dyke.
Give me a good doer without wind galls or vice.
Crupper that Clyde and fettle his feather
and keep somewhere in the kist the fate
of the foundered horse
and the meaning of names –
Breakheart Hill and Killhorse Lane.

Wood man

between Anchor
and New Invention, we left the Christmas

lights of the farms, climbed instead
a slippery stile, marked '*Danger*'

slipped into a narrow valley full of falling water
and took a faint path, weft to the birch trees'

warp, felt, underfoot, loose earth
unbound by ash and brook

found waiting round a corner, furred and green,
knuckle-fingered and splay-legged

reared up and rooted, chapel-lonely, a sightless
wodwo, somewhere on the border

Regarders of the forest

fluffed in frost, a robin sings high up
as sun low down
lays down on draggled moss

while at our feet below the chestnut bough
the emptied chestnut cases hedge
& hog through leaf mould

here step the beasts of the chase, namely
the buck, the doe, the fox
the marten & the roe

this day in Sallow Coppice, we are late-come
regarders of the forest,
witnesses of waste
& assart, purpresture

here's forest law, protect the vert, protect
the oaks, protect the lesser trees,
the hazel, elder, sallow,
on which the deer may feed

December, & the deer fruits nibbled down
then at our snapped twigs
the does will lift their heads

& turn long eyes to stare
rise to run, their pelted
shoulders touching
as they flit this wood

the wandering court brings justice
for offence against the venison,
the dog-draw & the stable-stand
the back-bear & the bloody-hand

our ears catch bleat of hungry sheep
four fields away
& cars hum
all around this wood

while under soil the Saxon Mocktree Forest
surges under Weo Edge,
beneath Stoke Wood
it leaves a trace

old hunting ground that noses down
the Onny, scents along the Teme
& runs the hart
through Bringewood Chase

Heart of Wales line

Onny waters, obedient
now back within their bounds

floods, drained out of woods
the washed earth

the swans arranged
like quiet china

between the trees, snowdrops
spread like tablecloths

Her maps, their annotations

Nothing but the flat pour of river water
that erases her.

The bared trees. The contour lines
of crocus bulbs washed out.

Her fine straight hair.
Her maps, their annotations.

I'm early by this brown-lit
roaring stream.

She's going further
every day.

I focus in the wind.
Her glasses in their case.

The cold eats in.
The battered daffodils.

The noise.

Craa-craa

New-old things, brought to my hand.
Sunday, a brass pin. Monday,
an earring. One week, a green bead.

sing black crow feather   white crow bone

When everything in the world
was made of new things, I
owned the gifts of crows.

Then-now it strides on wrinkled toes.
Head-tilt. Wait. Keen flick of eye.
Shuffle feathers. Hop.

sing black crow feather   white crow bone

Now my world's everything
is hollowed through: trickled by absence,
porous imestone hill.

In five crow-lives my gifts have worn away:
mislaid in house moves, slipped
through attic planks.

sing black crow feather   white crow bone

I owned the gifts
of a crow's wink
only on loan.

almanack iv

eosturmonath

in the month of opening –

what splits
what shits
what births
what widens
its eyes?

thrimilce

the month of three milkings
when the bull
sidling in his concrete pen
swings his horns
at our fingers

seremonath

the first travelling month
earth dried enough
to ring hollow under foot-weight
air warm enough
to fetch everything near

Westray Wifie

cock-eyed, hunched on cracked flags, she's blowsy
among the stones, the bones, the midden left
by cattle tied indoors through the long-nights
their bellies swollen, udders shrinking
ribs sharp as groynes at slack
through lack of fodder

propped so long on a throughstone
she leans over the tether-posts
over the hungry, sweltered cows

she is her belly, brought to bear

deep line of her brow, her wide
scratched eyes, her claw of ancient hair
her two high breasts, her broad haunch –

she draws the blood, brings milk, tugs spring

she'll see them through the dark
        to drop their calves
                at Noltland's inching
                        door of daylight

Fiddlers Causeway

What you knew was a lane between drystone walls,
that took the Hardland down to the Mosses.

What you knew was its steepness,
rolling with limestones big as a churn lid.

You could have forgotten the dairy herd lumbering,
full-bagged, weary, up to the farm.

You could have forgotten the stones that pressed
through the thin bendy soles of our wellies.

But do you hear the rush and stumble of their legs,
the press of piebald, the spattering of their shit?

Do you remember the wetness and dark of the lame
cow's eye as she hobbled up last on the causeway?

The loudest spring

Twelve midnight   and the gibbous moon's not up.
I walk the street in nailed boots
from skirts of orange light to thick-soled dark.

At the bang of a door I will go into a cat,
to slink the teeth of a garden fence,
to wash my paws on a stranger's mat.

Twelve midnight   and this birch tree's breathing.
I'll take a new leaf damply in each hand
hear its branches scrape at stars.

In the sill of a gutter I will go into a mouse,
rapid-eyed, thin-skinned and gnawing.
A tulip's black throat will be my house.

Twelve midnight   and toadflax meshes the gravel.
I crunch the stars in nailed boots.
The pavements are caving in.

In the nip of a gable I will go into a bat,
spin blind through the dark like a seed,
cry silence through the subsiding flats.

Twelve midnight   and tv aerials are stars.
I cast my spell. Plastics riddle the soil.
Cities starve out the earthworms.

In my nailed boots I will go into nothing,
will cheat the wide-open mouth of the dark;
will whistle up the loudest spring.

near Todleth

in a field of docks rain falls on us

here are white hanks of sheepswool
pegged like washing
between drying posts

we breathe in lanolin and damp

by clouded reeds a tatty ewe
her off-fore lame
lurches away with her twins

her bag all lumpy with mastitis

you said it wouldn't last
we follow
an orange tip butterfly over a stile

Not there, nearly
Old Church Stoke

This cream blackthorn warm of morning is the hour
to be patching the cattle trailer with squint squares
of corrugated tin and new rivets.

The air is lamb-bleat soft. Away up the lane go
steady hoofbeats, clip of iron to stone, the horse-pace
laid in layers over the land.

A tawny owl flies in daylight, has the wrong century.
Wings it straight and low and silent to the coppice,
and doesn't come out.

From a hedge three redstarts tilt at us, tails bright
with rust, backlit by sun, their voices
shrill then not.

They're only briefly there, same as the moat that's mostly
silted up. But here behind the wire that keeps apart
the barren arable and the green

gunpowder wood, the moat ghosts halfway round
its mound. Bluebells glimmer like a rumour.
The trees hide everything.

Dialects of the coppice

We have come to watch spring write itself
in lithoed tractor tyres.
The fluttering mark of Wood Whites
on the air is unpronounceable.

Here ambiguous deer leave in their mud
the occasional
quotation mark
then dash –

On the track the iron shoes of horses
press and pass.
The coppice boles are bold above
the lean italics of grass.

Pond prints out quivered sky.
We can't translate
its soaking scrip of weed.
The trees rephrase the words
the air has shed

and high in the ear we learn
the silences between
the notes of wrens.
Their pauses, language of reply.

The tattoo'd man

has had a skinful, to go only by what shows.
His bull neck's chained, a padlock swings
above its own hatched shadow.
In scrolling calligraphic script, his knife arm
pledges faith in love, and brags
his unsurrendered soul.

His other arm is tidal. On the backswell
of a bicep lolls a mermaid, tits
like limpets, eyes like stones.
An anchor lodges in the flesh above
his wrist: its taut rope twists
across his sturdy, sandy bones.

But much of him's of land, for deep
in the humus of his cheek
a splitting acorn roots.
An oak leaf grows towards
his mouth on sappy, pliant shoots.

With men, it's never easy to be sure, but
here's one who's tried to take the outside in.
He's shifty as gulls and bitter as bark.
Every night he reads thát skin:
his library of pain
and virtue, bright and thin.

Preseli

Zig-zag we leapt
                    reed island to tuft

and under us the wind flashed the pools.

The nervous sheep lurched up to plod away

and fog-rags
            swam the cairns of Foeldrygarn.

The horizon rose like a pockmarked moon.

In rain Beddarthur stones woke up
                                        and trod their place.

We saw a listening ring.

Sharpened our wits
                    stepped in.

One uncertain history

Wide horns and white
medieval flanks.
Heavy as sighs,
the park cattle linger
by a shrinking pool.

Bromesberrow, oaked, milky

I'm lit along the wood-edge.
Blond light off corn stubble,
a sky full of rain and light.
In one ear, press of hide on saplings,
the unseen deer retreat

Raggedstone, steep, sallow

A bellwether sheep
leads a long file past me,
roman nose to soiled tail.
They beat the cloven common
into the common

Hollybed, pale, trodden

Come out at the car park
red car, yellow car, sweet,
seedy blackberries.
Rain runs down me,
down the hill, and down the hour

The Gullet, fogged, viridian

The hills are always here.
They wear away.
They stay, grip close
the patience of the igneous.
Their fossils sit me out

Midsummer Hill, bedrock, bowl-sky

Banked with shades and shadows
winding up inside a slope
the deep lane remembers everything
forgets   remembers.
I misremember everything, I know

Chase End Hill, white cumulus, concrete trig

The not seen sea

Under cliff, under white chalk, Under Hooken
we walk down the throat of the harts tongue
and talk. Our boots are glossed with clever ivy.

Overgrown, overhead and soft under old man's beard,
bosomy June leans down on us, up close
to cyclical drift, centimetre shift of earth.

While, sunk in its cage of feathers, a blackbird rots,
deflates into the flint step down to the beach.
Shingle rumbles in our ears. It hisses, passes, as we

wind the path between the cliffs, and only now
and then we catch the hill-high lurch of chalk in mist.
Keen in the nose, the salt and fret of sea.

All the while we twist a flint descent by rungs
of ivy root, and all the while a thrush repeats
repeats its song to coil to coil inside our ears.

And another blackbird sings, so blackbird answers it
in audible waves. By our feet a chasm of ash and fog.
Low in our bones, not visible, churrs the sea.

In a fair field, at Whiteleaved Oak

The path was a thread through hills.
    Or the hazels galloped in wild garlic.

I had edged between white butterflies
    to get here, carrying lunch, and waterproofs.

I saw that the weight of long-dead feet had made
    this track, and bellied it, and smoothed its skin.

I was there below birds that sang in rings.
    Then the whole wood boomed under a plane.

A dog-walker walked, politely smiling by,
    and first a church bell called, and then a lamb.

Out of a green shade slopped the wash
    of warm shallow seas and a treasure of corals and crinoids

but now I idled on fired white clays, surprised
    when a trumpet sounded in a distant garden.

It fanned the black flies up to the contrails, so I sat down
    in the wrinkled field, and counted all those dandelion globes.

Notes

almanack i, ii, iii, iv – are shaped by the Old English months.

In yellowhammer weather – The Harp is a field in the parish of Clun. Polliwig was bred by Frank Collins of Clun Farm. The Yellowhammer says, 'A little bit of bread, and no cheese'.

this netted house – based on the sight of a derelict cottage entirely wrapped in fishing nets on the island of Lewis, with thanks to Emily Wilkinson.

Eliza in Lordshill after noon – the Baptist Chapel at Lordshill served the mining community of Brook Vessons.

Gabriel in Brook Vessons – Brook Vessons was a 19th century lead miners' squatter village below Stiperstones, now in ruins. It's close by the Baptist Chapel at Lordshill. woolert – an owl (Shropshire); jagger – packhorse driver (Shropshire).

How time is in fields - based on the field names of Acton Scott Farm in Shropshire, the 1839 Parish Map, and a long walk.

Fell daemon – native to Cumbria (as I am), the Fells worked as pack ponies, carrying lead, iron and charcoal over the high bridlepaths. Daemon - an inner or attendant spirit.

The bodger goes for a turn – The poppets are the two pieces of wood adjusted to take the length of the 'billet' the piece of wood that is to be turned. When they're knocked into the right place, they're in the 'bed' of the lathe. Tines, hoops and stails are the parts of a traditional rake.

Walker by Uley – For centuries the wool trade flourished in Uley and Dursley. The walker, or fuller, trampled wool cloth to clean and thicken it. There was a smallpox hospital on Downham Hill above Dursley.

A traveller from Uley to Owlpen enquires of landlord John Ferebee – based on a local story.

How strange we are – Henriette d'Angeville climbed Mont Blanc in 1838.

The horseman's word – was a secret initiation ceremony among horsemen in 19th century Scotland.

Regarders of the forest – *waste, assart, purpresture*: offences against the 1217 Charter of the Forest. Waste was the clearance of land, assart the creation of new arable and purpresture the enclosure of newly assarted land.
deer fruits : berries, seeds, nuts.
vert, venison, green-hew: the forest, the deer of the forest, the trees.
wandering court: the forest eyre, an itinerant court to enforce the Charter of the Forest.
The Regarders of the Forest were those employed to survey it and defend its interests.
The Mocktree Forest is in Shropshire.

Westray Wifie – The Neolithic figure of a woman carved in sandstone was found on the Links of Noltland, Orkney, in 2009.

Dialects of the Coppice – based on David Morley's suggestions about asemic writing.

Indigo Dreams Publishing Ltd
24, Forest Houses
Cookworthy Moor
Halwill
Beaworthy
Devon
EX21 5UU
www.indigodreams.co.